Welcome

Taylor Swift is a superstar like no other. She is the greatest songwriter of her generation, and one of the most exciting artists in the music industry today. From her career beginnings as a teen country starlet, to the genre-shifting global sensation she has become, Taylor's career has gone from strength to strength over the past two decades. She's unstoppable!

Now it's time to celebrate her amazing journey so far in creative style! In this book, you can unleash your inner artist and test your Swiftie knowledge. There are 36 Taylor-themed illustrations ready for you to customise with colour, plus a selection of fun puzzles to solve and quizzes to answer.

Are you ready for it? Then grab some colours and let's get started...

Contents

6 Colouring

Explore Taylor's amazing career so far through a collection of 36 illustrations. Customise them with colour however you like!

81 Activities

Solve puzzles and test your Swiftie knowledge with Taylor-themed quizzes

82 Escape the labyrinth

82 Spot the difference

83 Design Taylor's outfit

84 Wordsearches
   84 Albums
   86 Singles
   88 Taylor terms

90 Quizzes
   90 Easy
   92 Medium
   94 Hard

Colouring

Tick off the ones you've done!

9

11

15

17

21

23

27

29

33

35

39

41

A star is born

Taylor Alison Swift was born on 13 December 1989 in Pennsylvania. She started playing guitar and writing songs at the age of 12, hoping to become a country singer. After years of hard work and dedication Taylor eventually got a record deal. Her self-titled debut album was released in 2006.

Feeling lucky

Some people think the number 13 is unlucky, but not for Taylor – it's her favourite number! "I was born on the 13th. I turned 13 on Friday the 13th. My first album went gold in 13 weeks… Basically whenever a 13 comes up in my life, it's a good thing," she explained.

13

Country roots

Taylor's early albums featured a lot of country music influences, which was her favourite genre as a young teenager. She would often wear cowboy boots on stage to give her outfits a country look.

The Star-Spangled Banner

In the years before her huge world tours, some of Taylor's early performances were at sports events singing the national anthem. This helped to introduce her to a new audience outside of the country music scene.

Fearless

Taylor's second album, *Fearless*, was a huge success and made her famous. The lead single 'Love Story' became a Top 10 hit in many countries.

Fairytales

On her second album, Taylor often used themes of princes and princesses, romance and heartbreak in her lyrics and performances. The popular single 'Today Was a Fairytale' was later included as a bonus track on the re-recorded *Fearless (Taylor's Version)*.

Award-winner

In 2010, Taylor won her first Grammy Awards.
She picked up four trophies, including Album of
the Year for *Fearless*. At the time, she was the
youngest person to win that award in the entire
history of the Grammys.

Taylor's guitars

Taylor has used many different guitars over the years, and sometimes plays a banjo or ukulele, too. Early in her career, being a guitarist and songwriter helped her stand out from the other aspiring country singers.

Writing solo

After working with co-writers on her first two albums, Taylor wrote every song for *Speak Now* on her own. The record explored her growth from teenager to adulthood, and reflected on past relationships.

Add your favourite Taylor lyrics to the page and decorate them!

Share the love

During the Speak Now World Tour, Taylor popularised the heart-hand gesture. "The heart-hand symbol means something between 'I love you' and 'thank you'," she explained. "It's just a sweet, simple message that you can deliver without saying a word."

Ringleader

Taylor wore her iconic sequinned circus ringleader outfit when performing 'We Are Never Ever Getting Back Together' during The Red Tour.

The scarf

In the ballad 'All Too Well', Taylor sings about an old scarf that an ex-boyfriend kept long after their relationship ended. Fans have speculated for years about the meaning of the scarf, and who has it, but Taylor insists that it's just a metaphor!

Action!

As well as being a super-talented musician, Taylor
has appeared in several films and television shows
during her career. What's your favourite on-screen
Taylor performance?

Musical evolution

Taylor's musical style is always evolving, which is why it's always so exciting to find out what she will do next! Over the years, she has turned her hand to country, pop, electro, synth-pop, R&B, indie-folk and more!

Embracing the 80s

On her fifth studio album, *1989*, Taylor incorporated lots of musical styles and techniques from the decade she was born. Eighties music featured plenty of synthesisers, drum machines and creative vocals.

Swift style

As her music has evolved with each album, so has Taylor's fashion. From cowboy boots and ballgowns to retro jackets, cosy cardigans, sparkly jumpsuits and more – she never goes out of style!

A new look

At the 2016 Met Gala, Taylor debuted a bold new look. Her hair was bleached and her makeup was more gothic, with a dark lipstick instead of her usual red. The theme of the event that year was 'Fashion in an Age of Technology' – how will you style Taylor's futuristic dress?

Karyn the snake

During the Reputation Stadium Tour, Taylor's stage was decorated with lots of snakes, including a giant inflatable cobra called Karyn.

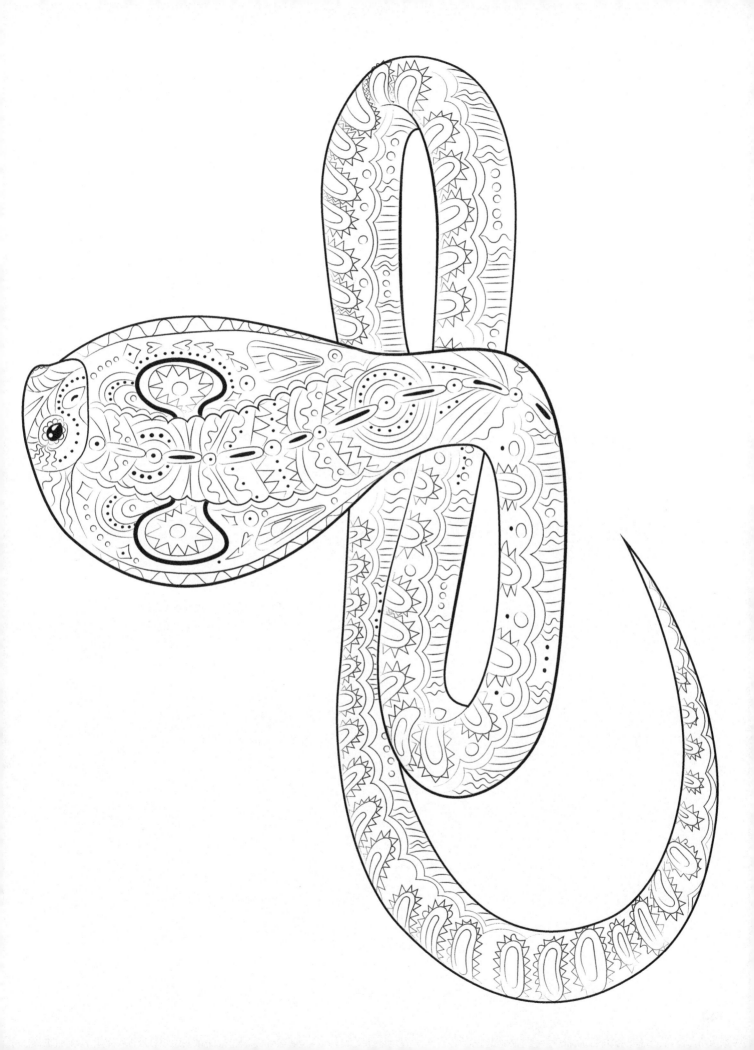

Giving back

Taylor has supported many different charities
and causes throughout her career. She also has a
reputation for making surprise donations to
fans and organisations in need.

Record-breaker

During her career so far, Taylor has repeatedly broken records for a variety of amazing accomplishments, including award wins, album sales, streaming totals and chart successes.

Purrrrrfect pets

Taylor loves cats! She has adopted two Scottish Folds – Olivia Benson and Meredith Grey, named after her favourite TV show characters – and a Ragdoll called Benjamin Button, named after the literary character.

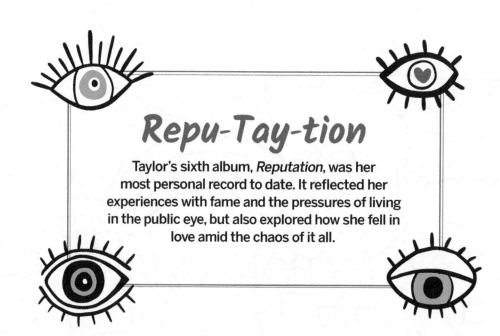

Repu-Tay-tion

Taylor's sixth album, *Reputation*, was her most personal record to date. It reflected her experiences with fame and the pressures of living in the public eye, but also explored how she fell in love amid the chaos of it all.

Activism

In recent years, Taylor has been using her fame to help raise awareness of different social and political issues. "I felt like I had to speak up to try and help make a change," she explained.

Spreading her wings

Taylor described her seventh album, *Lover*, as "a love letter to love". The album's colourful imagery and butterfly motifs represented her moving on and leaving the darker themes of *Reputation* behind.

Taking a stand

When the master copies of Taylor's first six albums were purchased against her will, she decided to take action. She has been re-recording the albums, from *Taylor Swift* to *Reputation*, and releasing new 'Taylor's Version' editions, which she owns the rights to.

Woman of the Decade

In 2019, Taylor became the first ever recipient of Billboard's Woman of the Decade award. She was given the title in recognition of her incredible musical accomplishments, as well as her charity and activism.

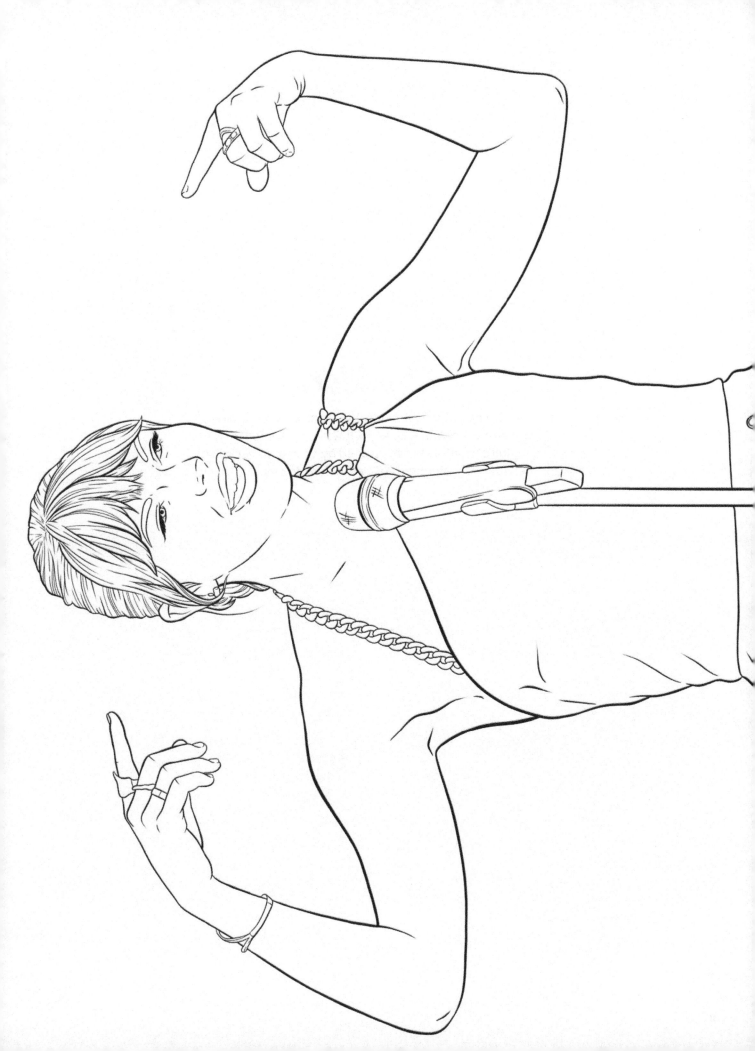

Folklore

In July 2020, Taylor delighted fans by announcing a surprise album – *Folklore*. It was an indie-folk record, full of wistful stories inspired by a need for escapism during the Covid-19 lockdowns.

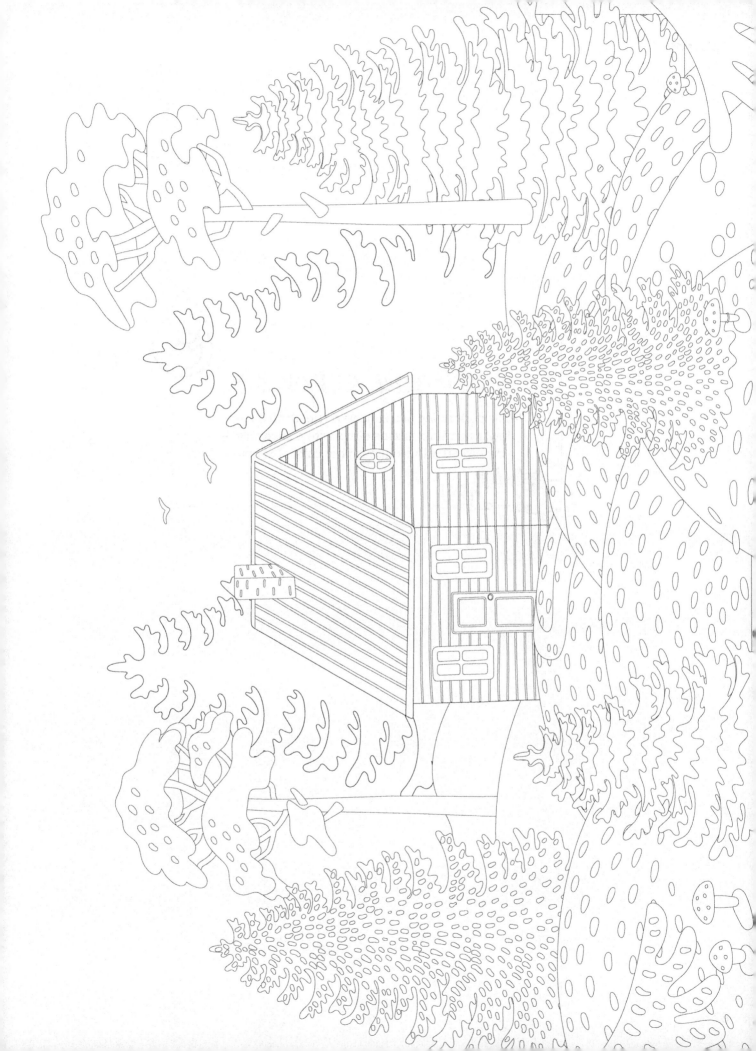

Birthday surprise!

While performing at a concert on her 30th birthday,
Taylor was surprised on stage with a huge cake –
decorated with pictures of her cats, of course!

Tyler Swift

The music video for 'The Man' focuses on the character of Tyler Swift – Taylor's male alter ego – and explores sexism and double standards faced by women. The end of the video reveals that Tyler is actually played by Taylor herself, under lots of clever prosthetics and make-up!

Indie sisters

In December 2020, Taylor released *another* surprise album, *Evermore*, just five months after *Folklore*. It was a continuation of her new indie sound – Taylor describes them as "sister albums".

Flower power

At the Grammy Awards in 2021, Taylor wore a beautiful dress covered in flowers. As the Covid-19 pandemic was ongoing, she also had a matching face mask – who says you can't be safe *and* stylish?

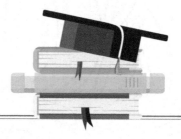

Con-graduations!

In May 2022, Taylor received an honorary doctorate
from New York University. She attended that year's
graduation ceremony and gave an inspirational
speech to the students.

Sleepless nights

Taylor said that her tenth album, *Midnights,* was "a collection of music written in the middle of the night". The electro-pop record is one of her most personal, exploring Taylor's anxieties and insecurities.

Super songwriter

Taylor's clever lyrics and storytelling abilities are what make her music so unique and fascinating. Her songwriting skills even earned her the Songwriter-Artist of the Decade Award in 2022.

Grammy glamour

In 2023, Taylor won the Grammy Award for Best Music Video for *All Too Well: The Short Film*, which she wrote and directed herself. It was based on the epic ten-minute extended version of the song from *Red (Taylor's Version)*.

The Eras Tour

Taylor's long-awaited 2023 tour is a celebration of all the different musical styles used throughout her career. The spectacular show is over three hours long, featuring 44 songs from all of her albums.

Activities

- [ ] **82** Escape the labyrinth
- [ ] **82** Spot the difference
- [ ] **83** Design Taylor's outfit

Wordsearches

- [ ] **84** Albums
- [ ] **86** Singles
- [ ] **88** Taylor terms

Quizzes

- [ ] **90** Easy
- [ ] **92** Medium
- [ ] **94** Hard

✔ Tick off the ones you've done!

Labyrinth

Taylor has lost her cats! Help her navigate the labyrinth to find them

Spot the difference

Can you find the FIVE changes made to the image on the right?

Taylor-made

Design a new dress for Taylor's next event!

Wordsearch

Can you find these nine studio album titles in the puzzle?

```
Y  Z  Q  D  M  A  D  F  Z  P  Y  B  F  T  L
Y  G  P  W  A  R  M  I  S  A  N  V  C  F  R
P  V  K  C  P  F  X  M  M  I  L  G  W  I  R
K  R  A  C  E  R  O  M  R  E  V  E  F  W  R
Y  A  Z  M  I  D  N  I  G  H  T  S  O  S  E
P  Z  S  J  L  J  G  C  P  F  S  L  L  R  P
T  O  Y  Q  J  I  R  X  H  E  P  J  K  O  U
W  W  W  U  Z  P  D  E  R  A  T  N  L  L  T
L  F  O  H  A  O  K  D  R  R  Y  L  O  Y  A
Y  A  L  N  D  C  V  Q  Z  L  B  E  R  A  T
C  J  C  R  K  K  A  L  S  E  J  C  E  T  I
P  H  W  S  E  A  J  N  E  S  B  X  Z  Q  O
C  K  E  L  O  V  E  R  E  S  D  H  B  K  N
V  Y  E  V  A  Y  S  P  F  K  B  T  J  F  P
W  J  G  B  V  M  T  F  S  E  C  R  K  P  S
```

Find these words...

TAYLORSWIFT	RED	FOLKLORE
FEARLESS	REPUTATION	EVERMORE
SPEAKNOW	LOVER	MIDNIGHTS

Wordsearch

Find the names of Taylor's singles
hidden in this word jumble...

```
I F P W Y V S P W T W R R N M
T E F N O B J R S T Y D E A B
L W E O B B J T J Z Q F D A V
L T O E T N Z C E X J F S Q X
E N H L V I T O R E H I T N A
W N A E L C E M P U W Y E L L
O K B G M I W K Z J Q U O K D
O Y C V I A W Z A G T V M R R
T X U J Y D N R G H E T I B O
L V Q T Z C R D R S S U N M U
L X G R O S G A T C R O E F R
A O H F J K V O C D K Z F W T
T M I C T I R O F Y D A E R G
W B U D M Y U F G R I U O G H
W W A R G C M M I T H J O L Y
```

Find these words...

MINE	TIMMCGRAW	READYFORIT	WILLOW
RED	LOVESTORY	THEMAN	ALLTOOWELL
	SHAKEITOFF	CARDIGAN	ANTIHERO

Wordsearch

Can you find all the Taylor-themed
words hidden below?

```
Y T V J N U M O D B S X Z X M
O S A P D Q N I M A J N E B E
L A T Y K E W G K Q H I P Q A
I R D Z L Q I R R T X O Q P O
V E X T B O C R J Y Z R E F E
I T L H A X R B U J M D J E C
A S S I O H W S I P R H O I O
H Y F R B N Y H V I J J L T B
T N Y T B O N U Y E R Y K F E
I H B E Q C T P Z G R U E I D
D T X E D I S U A I G S T W L
E I A N I S K F C F J L I S G
R B A N N V L S Z F N L R O U
E A U R G G E R E T S A E N N
M R E D X S S T Q B F R X T G
```

Find these words...

TAYLORSVERSION   THIRTEEN   ICON   BENJAMIN
EASTEREGG   LYRICS   OLIVIA
ERAS   SWIFTIE   MEREDITH

Quiz

Easy

1. **What is Taylor's middle name?**
- [ ] Alison
- [ ] Betty
- [ ] Marjorie
- [ ] Dorothea

2. **What was the title of her debut album?**

_____

3. **What year was she born?**

_____

4. **Complete the lyric:**
"It's a love story, baby,

_____ "

5. **What is Taylor's lucky number?**

_____

6. **Which of her albums was the first to be re-recorded as a 'Taylor's Version'?**

_____

7. **Which of these instruments can Taylor play?**
- [ ] Guitar
- [ ] Piano
- [ ] Banjo
- [ ] All of the above

8. **What is the name of her 2023 tour?**

_____

9. **Which US state did Taylor move to as a teenager to pursue her music career?**

_____

10. **Taylor has won over 500 awards during her career**
- [ ] True
- [ ] False

Taylor Swift

Quiz
Medium

1. Which of Taylor's first ten studio albums is missing from the wordsearch on page 85?

_____

2. How old was Taylor when her first single was released?

_____

3. Which three songs on *Folklore* explore a love triangle from each person's perspective?

_____
_____
_____

4. How tall is Taylor?

_____

5. Who provided the voice for Taylor's male alter ego Tyler Swift in the music video for 'The Man'?

_____

6. Which rapper infamously interrupted Taylor's acceptance speech at the 2009 VMAs?

_____

7. Complete the lyric: *"You call me up again just to*

_____

_____ *"*

8. What are the names of Taylor's three cats?

_____
_____
_____

9. What is the title of Taylor's autobiographical documentary released in 2020?

_____

10. Taylor has an animal species named after her

☐ True   ☐ False

Quiz

Hard

1. What was Taylor's first number one single on the Billboard Hot 100?

   _____

2. In 2019, Taylor broke the Guinness World Record (previously held by Michael Jackson) for winning the most of which award?

   _____

3. Which singer was Taylor named after?

   _____

4. Complete the lyric: *"Did you hear my covert narcissism,*

   _____ *"*

5. What Swedish pseudonym (fake name) has Taylor previously used as a songwriter?

   _____

6. Joe Alwyn also co-wrote songs under a fake name on *Folklore* and *Evermore*, what was it?

   _____

7. Who did Taylor duet with on the track *'The Last Time'*?

   _____

8. In 2021, Taylor wrote and directed the short film *All Too Well* based on her song of the same name. Which actors starred in the two lead roles?

   _____

   _____

9. What was the name of the contest-winning poem that Taylor wrote when she was ten?
   - ☐ Pen in My Hand
   - ☐ Monster in My Closet
   - ☐ Pebble in My Shoe
   - ☐ Gum in My Hair

10. Who can be heard at the very beginning of *'Gorgeous'*?

    _____

Answers

Labyrinth

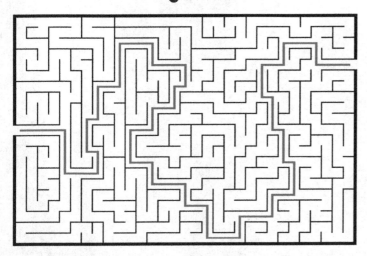

Spot the difference

Wordsearches

Albums

Singles

Taylor terms

Quizzes

Easy

1. Alison
2. *Taylor Swift*
3. 1989
4. "Just say yes", from 'Love Story'
5. 13
6. *Fearless*
7. All of the above
8. The Eras Tour
9. Tennessee
10. True

Medium

1. 1989
2. 16
3. 'Cardigan', 'August' and 'Betty'
4. About 5ft 10in, or 1.78m
5. Dwayne Johnson
6. Kanye West
7. "Break me like a promise" from 'All Too Well'
8. Meredith Grey, Olivia Benson and Benjamin Button
9. *Miss Americana*
10. True – a millipede called Nannaria swiftae

Hard

1. 'We Are Never Ever Getting Back Together'
2. American Music Award (AMA)
3. James Taylor
4. "I disguise as altruism" from 'Anti-Hero'
5. Nils Sjöberg
6. William Bowery
7. Gary Lightbody
8. Sadie Sink & Dylan O'Brien
9. Monster in My Closet
10. James Reynolds – the daughter of Blake Lively & Ryan Reynolds

* Quiz answers correct as of April 2023

TAYLOR SWIFT
COLOURING & ACTIVITY BOOK

Future PLC Quay House, The Ambury, Bath, BA1 1UA

Editorial
Editor **Jacqueline Snowden**
Senior Designer **Harriet Knight**
Senior Art Editor **Andy Downes**
Head of Art & Design **Greg Whitaker**
Editorial Director **Jon White**

Illustrations
Kym Winters

Contributors
Dan Peel

Cover images
Alamy, Getty Images, Kym Winters

Photography
Alamy, Getty
All copyrights and trademarks are recognised and respected

Advertising
Media packs are available on request
Commercial Director **Clare Dove**

International
Head of Print Licensing **Rachel Shaw**
licensing@futurenet.com
www.futurecontenthub.com

Circulation
Head of Newstrade **Tim Mathers**

Production
Head of Production **Mark Constance**
Production Project Manager **Matthew Eglinton**
Advertising Production Manager **Joanne Crosby**
Digital Editions Controller **Jason Hudson**
Production Managers **Keely Miller, Nola Cokely,
Vivienne Calvert, Fran Twentyman**

Printed in the UK

Distributed by Marketforce, 5 Churchill Place, Canary Wharf, London, E14 5HU
www.marketforce.co.uk – For enquiries, please email:
mfcommunications@futurenet.com

Taylor Swift Colouring & Activity Book First Edition (MUB4823)
© 2023 Future Publishing Limited

FUTURE Connectors.
Creators.
Experience
Makers.

Future plc is a public   Chief Executive Officer **Jon Steinberg**
company quoted on the   Non-Executive Chairman **Richard Huntingford**
London Stock Exchange   Chief Financial and Strategy Officer **Penny Ladkin-Brand**
(symbol: FUTR)
www.futureplc.com   Tel +44 (0)1225 442 244

Widely
Recycled

ipso. For press freedom
with responsibility

Made in the USA
Las Vegas, NV
28 November 2023